Shaking Music
from the
Angry Air

Shaking Music from the Angry Air © 2025 Michael Dwayne Smith

Cover art: LaWanda Walters

ISBN: 978-1-962405-23-2
Library of Congress Control Number: 2025938582

Sheila-Na-Gig Editions
Russell, KY
Hayley Mitchell Haugen, Editor
www.sheilanagigblog.com

Shaking Music
from the
Angry Air

poems

Michael Dwayne Smith

Sheila-Na-Gig Editions

Advance Praise

Michael Dwayne Smith's *Shaking Music from the Angry Air* is an ultra-rich, self-revelatory and confessional tapestry of familial alcoholic disturbances, youthful desert desires, disappointments and starlit joy, a wolf howl through the chaos of growing up in unforgiving Southern California dreamscapes and Mojave mirage. The entire collection, Smith's fourth, is buttressed throughout on masterfully crafted language, a scaffolding of humor, pathos, sexiness, cigarettes, lust and rust. The imagery and metaphors are deft and potent, daring, deliciously surprising, with sentences that read like smooth aged Scotch, crisp and wild, surreal, funny and bittersweet by turns, with tales of girls, women, and male longing sketched with vivid colors, riding on wild horses, falling into potent remorse. This is a damned serious collection of dazzling poems, each of which arrests the reader's soul and never releases it from their grasp.

—**Jeffrey Bryant**, author of *The Catacombs of Vanished Lovers*

Michael Dwayne Smith's collection, *Shaking Music from the Angry Air*, is a tough, muscular ride. Grit your teeth, hold tight. Love and death loom even as you find "little tides and pools of promise" to somehow buoy you. This is a story of orange groves, warm beer, lust, and living through stuff to witness "distant laments, strange and precious." You're "dying upward" while "finding beauty in the breakdown." This is a ride you'll remember.

—**Carolyn Adams**, author of *Going Out to Gather*

I enjoy reading and rereading Michael Dwayne Smith's excellent poetry in *Shaking Music from The Angry Air*. In one poem he says, "My words make a ceiling I keep revising." I feel that I stand under that ceiling, marveling at it. The poems often root deeply in memory. Many make reference to California. Smith can paint a sad situation, but moments of humor impact and surprise us. This book is a joy.

—**Kenneth Pobo**, author of *At the Window, Silence*

Michael Dwayne Smith's new collection opens with a stunner of a poem, loaded with vivid imagery and sharp, pointed observations and phrases that twist and surprise the reader. Smith manages to keep the intensity and freshness alive in his collection, spanning the sprawling California landscape whether in the streets of Los Angeles, the isolation of the Mojave Desert, or the lonely highways that lead to divergent points on the map and connect the flawed humans that inhabit that world. These poems offer a kaleidoscope of colors, images, and metaphors that startle. There is a sense of loss and hope, regret and delight, with an overriding layer of compassion and humor. In turn, surreal, compassionate, humorous, hopeful, and heartbreaking, these poems will stay with you. As Smith says in his poem "Maybe, Maybe", *There's a kind of immortality to my dreams.*

—**Michael Minassian**, author of *Jack Pays a Visit* and *1000 Pieces of Time*

This poetry burns with energy, urgency, and an unflinching honesty that won't let you look away. Each piece in *Shaking Music from the Angry Air* is a heartbeat, a protest, a submission woven with sharp perspective and raw emotions. Just when you think the work becomes too heavy, his words crack open a sliver of light, an "ah-ha" moment, a spark of humor. These are poems that demand your attention.

—**Linda Goin**, author of *She-Oak*

Acknowledgments

Some poems in this collection appeared in earlier versions, sometimes under a different title. The author gratefully acknowledges the support of editors for the following publications:

Bending Genres: "Maybe, Maybe"

Book of Matches: "Backyard Beers and Thoughts with Two Jocular Dogs," "Every Damn Thing," "No Elegance," "Poem Ending with a Barry Humphries Quote"

Chiron Review: "April and October," "Healing"

Cholla Needles Literary Journal: "Dear Mother, Do You Recall," "High School Project," "Inevitable," "Poem Ending with a Line by Frank O'Hara," "Poem in which I Survive," "The Five Fires"

Disturb the Universe: "Bliss Feels Like Shit," "Intervals and Rhythms," "It had taken two years, the last two"

Ethel: "Muse," "Poem with Little Riffs…"

FRiGG: "The Entrepreneur and His Fortunes," "This Sunday Feeling," "We Cover Our Heads from Light"

Gargoyle: "Grief is a Coat"

Gyroscope Review: "Come From the Blinding Light and Hear"—nominated for Best of the Net

Heavy Feather Review: "Osculation"

Hole in the Head Review: "Art Made from Happiness is Shit," "Let's Crash"

Home Planet News: "All Those Ideals of Rivera's," "At Sixty, a Young Woman…," "Weathered"

Impostor: A Poetry Journal: "Poem Ending with a Line from Luc Besson's Lucy"

Medusa's Kitchen: "Divinations,""Ghost Chasing," "I'll Ask to Walk Her Home," "Lost Letter to Emily," "Night Whispers," "Slow Studies," "The Fall Approaches"

ONE ART: A Journal of Poetry: "Politic"

Phantom Kangaroo: "Love Smashed Us"

San Pedro River Review: "Alison," "Forgive Me, Father, for I"

Sheila-Na-Gig online: "A Kind of Hum," "Messenger without Umbrella"
The Orchards Poetry Journal: "Diminishment," "In Bed with Time and Fire"
Third Wednesday: "Horse Sense"
Trailer Park Quarterly: "Racing to the End"
Verse Virtual: "Notes on the Transitory Nature of Things"
Whiskey Paper: "Jupiter Moon Birds"—nominated for a Pushcart Prize

This book came together because of extraordinary support. First and foremost, I must, from my heart of hearts, thank everyone at Sheila-Na-Gig Editions, especially editor Hayley Mitchell Haugen, for believing in its worthiness, and for all the joy, craft, and inspiration brought to the poetry community at large (here I bow, with utmost respect).

Next, I must bring love for fellow poets Michael Minassian and Linda Goin. We three have met monthly for almost two years now, reading and critiquing our poems—many in this collection evolved during those sessions; they also read versions of this manuscript. Both are gracious, honest, and wise in their criticism. Sláinte, dear poet friends!

I'd also like to thank the following brilliant poets for their support in reading this manuscript: Ellyn Maybe, Tim Suermondt, Pui Ying Wang, Donna Hilbert, Kenneth Pobo, Jeffrey Bryant, Carolyn Adams, and Jennifer Glover—you have my love forever!

Most importantly, infinite love and gratitude to my family—Bonnie, Evan, Lili, Liam—without whom this world would be unbearable.

To every "boy" out there muscling through
a family of addicts, striving to define love, spirit,
and family, sacrificing the identity of expectation
for the many selves of reconciliation.

Table of Contents

III. *Counterweight to a vast, sad, damned world*

IV. *A distant wind-chime jitters*

"What brings order in the world is to love
and let love do what it will."
                                        —Krishnamurti

I. How shall I wear my identity?

Angelitas

Guaymas, Mexico, 1968: the June sun falls
on my angry skin like a lick of fire, and the
cactus by our beach camp drowses, heavy.
No birds grace the sleeping sky, but my father,
elephantine, rasping, gripping his Coors like
the Grail, lunges this way and that, barking
drill-sergeant serious for order. *God dammit,
Anita, can't this kid…* his litany trailing onto
the long, empty shore, spilling into the Pacific.
Back home there is Viet Nam, Chicago, LSD.
Hippies and Panthers stalk Ozzie and Harriet.

Here things are usual, unchanged. Mother's
drunk by noon, father's fist never unfolds,
my dirty locks beat in the wind. I slip away,
run toward the hungry arms of the ocean,
flapping my awkward feet across the sand—
there are coals between my toes and blisters
break out like tiny white mushrooms on my
quick pink flesh. There is perfect company
in this absence of people, and the breakers fan
along the edge of boundlessness. What is this
power pulling the ground out from under me?
It towers fitfully, collapsing to bury the bones
of its own, absent of shape or logic or love.

From further up, I see a tiny figure, growing
larger, racing at the water. A local boy, older
than me, maybe thirteen, and he smiles, brown
muscle gleaming as he sprints. *Ola!* he cries,
and he launches himself into the surf, as if it
were glad to have him. He gives himself over.
I stop, watch him flip through waves: farther,
farther out he swims, arching back to the sun,
as I stare, amazed, his stringy limbs cutting

seams in the sea. And then come the screams...
they spring up sharp from the bay, terrible and
piercing, an animal cry from a place in his gut
deeper than any god could go. He erupts from
the foam, furious legs and knotting tendon, as his
sleek body buckles, contracting, falling to shore,
blue stingers of maybe a hundred jellyfish lashed
to his chest. I remember heat, those tiny whips,
a full confirmation of faith. I remember the fear
in his eyes, how I didn't move, couldn't speak.
He was in the order now. *Bienvenido, hermano.*

What I Fear to Write Tracks Me Down

Today I am a bear. My snout is wet, and I lurk
in your woods, my belly and the faint scent of you
moving my muscular legs and paws. Sway
away from poachers. Wade. Bear trap

in the berries, glinting. I'll go into town tonight
to satisfy my garbage heart, drag my matted
black fur, rush raccoons, startle fawn and
deer and half-drunk husbands— invincible with

stupid shotguns and shouts. You'll see my
moody eyes in the dark. In your yard. I'll be
trespassing your property. You'll lock the doors.
I'll catch an ear on the rusted nail of your flimsy

wooden fence. Will I kill your cat. Your dog.
Or be satisfied with the freezer-burned love you
tossed out last night. Don't wax about the moon
reflected on my shiny coat. I am not your pelt.

The last breath you smell may be mine, lush
with rotting teeth and bloody tongue, throat
slathered and stomach rumbling to the droll roll
of your puny pulse. Don't bury bones in the yard.

Don't try to hide.

Footwork

My father leaned on bars like
>   Nureyev tipped on floors.
>>   It was a certain grace: a red
>   rag body
slipped and poured into
>   furniture—
fixed or laughing, pissed or dancing,
>   the little shit could flick a jab with his left
>   quicker'n you could think.
It was goddam
>   ballet: spin around the stools and
>   work the crowd,
jokes and hands and pinch an ass
>   and here the drinks'd come. "Flatter
the fat woman, flirt with
>   the fag in the overdone eyes,"
>>   Dad would say as
King-For-A-Day, scotch and blowjobs for life,
>   bobbing and weaving,
>>   flipping the pages
of his encyclopedic brain, where he'd recorded
>   every racist joke
>   he'd ever heard,
but trading one drink for three
>   was his specialty. "Always buy
>>   first,"
he'd tell me, "Serve with bullshit buddy-speak
>   and machismo drool."
>>   And just to keep the
>   timing right, he'd kick up
the occasional fight. "Keeps gas in the tank,
>   n' smoke in the eye," he'd say.

That scorched day I busted his face,
>   reeling around
>   from behind the rust-red pump
at a Vegas filling station,

he dropped to the pavement and smiled
      like I'd arrived. He leaped to his feet,
paid cash for the fuel,
      and in the viscous heat,
for the first time in years, he called me
      Son. The toothless
          attendant laughed
in the swirling sand, waved the ragged bills
      as we sped away,
and in the red of the blood
      of my father's eye,
I saw the sad choreography of it all: one
      movement making necessary the next,
          the hard logic
of ignorant pain,
the strained chorus of loss, the tragic gravity
      of cuts and glass and falling down
      drunk, of stinking sex—
we drove for hours without a word.

We met again in Barstow, a few years down
      the road, at a gritty lounge
          from a shitty noir film,
his face a relief in shadow and stone.
      He had the cancer then,
          but didn't know.
Mother traveled with him,
      drinking gin, alone, again—
a trembling rabbit, in the tattered corner booth.
She watched, shitfaced,
      seated in yet another
          smoke and dim theater,
the kind of sordid nightly stage where he'd
      endlessly performed.
          The old man
was artful, knew his audience well. He had
      learned to lean his bones into a
          carcinogen wind and dance,
and dance, until his shadow took him home.

Love Smashed Us

We spin in our little boy beds. Top speed: imperceptible, inevitable, waiting to be split. Collided. Exploding into world. Veering off into steamy nights of future, disappearing, one blue molecule at a time.

Slick pages under my mattress ignite. Energy, release, repeat— obsession consumes a red licorice effigy. My charred lips will stencil black kisses over six hundred salty miles of flesh, of curves, and suspense. We shall be the polluting of sad girls rescued from small town bars, the liquor of one last hope, fuel burning into gravitational collapse.

Sleep is a paper boat. I'm soggy with memory. Fog creeps over the ocean, event horizon, and I am, or am not fusion, and I wake or soon imagine I wave toward a far shore, breaking against an imprint of stars on the rocks that rock in the sway of cooling planets and tides, floating upside down and backward, beneath my very own particle-thin slice of inverted yellow moon.

Are we still in bed? I can feel the quantum space my organs used to fill. Oxygen under blankets. I think about good health, the good life, but can't paint a likeness. And wonder about love, but don't try to hide in anyone's quiet, or cigarette-lit darkness. Green glowing eye of carbon monoxide alarm, you comfort me more than you could ever know.

Slow Studies

Flush with the idea of ripening,
we rode our bikes to school and
floated in crowded pools, chlorine
in our hair and mouths—

warmth and sweetness swayed
beneath palms, stupid ideas about
love swapped between us with tiny
kisses, and some mornings

were green, others rosy, until a heat
wave of afternoon touch, until light
from the sky died into imagination
and nibbles and fumbling

next to one another, me a stack of
firewood, you a small brush fire out
in the field behind the drug store
waiting, waiting with a

moon's eye on me, me skinny-legged,
all uncertain future, alone with the
thought of your blossoming flame,
hotter and hotter by degrees,

lips lining a fruited bowl for my bird
tongue, trill of chats and robins our
soundtrack, some Al Green mixed in,
a little hand-in-hand to begin,

then a language revealed by flesh,
texture, scent, aroma of plum flower,
everything pink and bruise, and it's
my birthday, naked in this

marooned spring of ripening, and
we burn it all down to feel ourselves
squeezed from the wet womb of
an inferno we'll never contain.

To a Murdered Boyhood Neighbor

No brilliantly colored macaws in the photo, only the
wire of the aviary, then your head,
inclined slightly backward.

Later that summer, some men shot you. Other people
threw you in an ambulance, the morgue, a grave.

I confess, my feeling barely noticed your grim end,
though we were neighbors,
though we exchanged uneasy banter

in the splintered days and homes of mutual friends.

I hated you. Hated you with virgin purity, wished
to trembling you would die, as lonely and miserable
as I felt to be alive.

Exploring memory, I find your burned-out cage.
Seems on the days I see you in that photograph,
a devastating crash occurs. You are wreckage

twisted to cold fossil in your younger age. You are fear
clawing out from under desperate plumage,
boney talons pressing a blade to my little dove throat.

You unfolded the grand theatrical wings of a death
you would years later unwittingly become.

So, you will never read this poem—
and no one else can understand it, my words just dirty
feathers and lice, molted, disease escaping on air.

We survivors resist, like monoliths, a desire to fly.
We pretend not to be exhausted from watching the

blackened nonsense of birds being hatched and dying.

Alison

Smell of fresh-plucked lemon, braided
scent of citrus and grazing horses and the back
of your neck in mid-afternoon.

Impasto-green fruit tree leaves
sticking to every scene,
San Gabriel Valley breeze a brushstroke
on the little brown curl of hair behind your ear.

The road in and the road out the same.

Northside train tracks in mud, dust in my hat.
Sleepy highway at grove's edge,
sometimes the orange summer foothills

on fire, sunset
whirling around the dirt path, you spinning
and spinning in that orange-blossom print dress

your mother sewed you, nimble, near dancing,
the valley flooding with calm,
my hands, tart fingers, my history and being,
the dry mouth of my future

all fallen out of fear, my heart unwashed.
Creaky wood house, straw-tinted at sunrise,
leaning slightly southward,

my blanket melancholy for your heat,
for the shape of you,
me hungry for the pink grapefruit of your mouth.

The road in and the road out the same.

Once-sweet groves, like me, like the lake
nearby, have soured in drought,
but I do still spin at the thought of us, and every
highway, every fire, still runs to you.

Jupiter Moon Birds

We used to put on the night pretty
& play until early,
lace & slow-burn graveyard shifters.

We were impossible to forgive,
all our voices bitter,
spoiled buttermilk to the tongue,

because we were loud secrets,
even unto ourselves,
spilled or spit out, cut & pasted

like dirty paper stars
on black particle-board,
bad high school science projects

bereft of serious logic,
rational only in the way Serenity taught us
to love three a.m. cupcake bakes

& swirling gin.

We scavenged each other's floors.
We were sick with sex & red knees & rancid breath.

Like all drunks we came to solemnity.

I found Serenity that way—
gold-sequin sneakers, candied cherries,
voice a smooth Guinness black,

found her in daylight,
exhausted, the bottles, too,
in the orange orchestrations

of an up & down sun,
& in the dozy stutter of planets
a feeling spread like absence,

only it wasn't absence,
but somehow little tides & pools
of promise, of dream confessionals,

somehow halfway to waking,
to whisper, & we were
walking like birds on a Jupiter moon.

Not to Nourish the Delusion

Downstairs, shrieks, too much Tequila and beer,
everything bumps and laughter. The night is icing over,
the talking's just begun.

Whoever knows a book best leads the discussion.
I listen to the heater tick in my room, exhale its
breath of fire. Someone chatters about acorns to

squirrels, someone else about Thoreau to rapturous,
half-drunk grad school girls,

all of us small in our rooms, but think we'll add up
to something, later. An outpouring of stars seems certain.
Against sand, and black density.

Out the apartment window, it's a blue night dome—
dogs skirt around a throw of pure halogen light.

The writer worries about freedom. Squirrels avoid
counting the calories in their nuts. I think about
my brother, sleeping it off in a Salvation Army shelter.

Our havens recede the faster we drink and sleep,
the faster the weather gets cold, and slows.
I'm shaking as hard as I can without being noticed.

I'm dancing like the other shoe is dropping, to save us all.
Nothingness feels clean. Stars, like the megalith of home.

These books make discussion. The Mothers of Invention
made records. My words make a ceiling I keep revising,
and raising, or I'll never get closer. Close enough for

a sleeping star to drink me, drunk enough to be frozen,
screaming laughter through to its stellar core.

All Those Ideals of Rivera's

Some mornings break free, inexplicably, like unguarded prison gates, and there he goes, a what-we-can-accomplish-together conversation machine, so certain he's repairing everything he broke yesterday. In his teens, he pissed on walls—school, police station, museum, hospital, library, church. Painted murals and talked to Diego in his head. Walls didn't matter. Separation did. He taunted barricades, danced atop the cinderblock that corralled neighbors' homes. It was better than a movie-house matinee, all those candid backyard snapshots. He glued the Polaroids to his parents' rooftop, a mosaic only he and God and a few Cessna pilots could view. From up in the air, we look all get-along, related, familial. Eye to eye, we be all racist, rapist, murderous. How to hide our bodies. But they're so heavy full of brokenness. To drag them out. To hop the wall. Give ourselves up, cop a plea to what seems fixable.

A Change in Climate

Here I am walking home from your place after your brother
trashed my Kia with his baseball bat. For as long as I can

remember, I wanted to live by the beach, a sandy pad with
open windows everywhere, people in and out like fads.

An artist's life, as in sleeping in and staying up, asking what's
next to love. Gratitude overwhelms me. True fact: today is

the best day for a person since ever, no matter some people
still cannot swim, and believe me nobody frets over thunder

storms like I do. The best sort of prayer is listening to one
another. Still, it won't keep an earthquake from collapsing

a City of Angels. Lately, seems the whole life thing is blurred,
our futures streaked with daubs of ammunition and eulogy,

so much that I quit writing songs about us, traded my guitar
for a baggie full of shrooms. You let me hold you, took me

in by the sea— I ate you out every night, yet you washed
away with the tide. Now the weight of three leagues drowns

my tongue. I can't speak or even whistle anymore. Don't
worry though. Scientists say it's too late to save us anyway.

That's How You Know

One night it comes over you. Sweet Love,
in a language you've never heard before.
A language this poem can speak. You know
what I mean. Love, Sweet Love. You just

know. I mean, it's not like your family knew
how to show Love, so, honestly, you can't be
sure exactly, exactly sure what Love looks or
feels like, but still. You know, right? This

has to be it. I mean, it's weird how you can't
think of anyone or anything else, to the point
of worry, even. You know? Like, what if this
person leaves. Fucking rips out your heart,

just like that. Or worse—what if this person
stays, and it's the woeful mistake of your life.
I mean, what if we're talking sociopath here.
I mean, how would *you* know. Your old man

went to prison for beating your mom, herself
batshit looney-tunes even before she started
drinking. So, who can be sure exactly, exactly
sure about this stuff. Best to play it safe. Love

is safe, right? I mean, Love is supposed to be
comforting and all, not risky or fearful, so
play it safe. You want to play it, but safely.
I mean, that's how you know that it's Love.

American Love Story

It was that kind of afternoon.

I flagged down the mailman, who said,
Sorry, still no more unemployment checks,
so I said, Take a break—
      let's get drunk on my couch and watch Ellen.

She said yes, that her injected
hormones burned, her tits ached,
that government pensions won't be
                what they used to be.

The TV made kissing a bore,
so we humped like scotch bunnies do
at closing time
      against wet alley dumpsters
inside a sulfurous and empty self-enlightenment.

After, we spooned on the shag carpet, ice
tinkling in sweaty glasses like
      trailer park chimes aroused by the memory
of a wicked Oklahoma twister
      and I confessed I was glad she kept the junk.

Before long, another boner watching Ellen
      bend over, ass audacious
in the camera lens, then I
got up and strolled naked to the kitchen
for cold beers, standing in front

of the open fridge, eyes closed, cooling down my
only-very-slightly-less-than-the-average-
      American-dude-sized erection.

I heard the mailman ask if my bathroom
      is transgender friendly. Of course, I said,
I take it like I give it... any way I can.

Stargazer

I was late for my Hollywood Psychic
appointment, a lady hypnotically
Caucasian and amiably medicated.

She says she was raised on love, but
I was raised on survival, so we see things
different. I told her my life's surrounded

by an incumbrance of old crows,
that I miss a regularity of astonishment.
She asked, Out in the shadows you roam

have you met any Mysterious Beings?
I said I hadn't. She pointed at her
bodycam, so I fessed up: there was a

gorgeous, pipe-smoking, desert bobcat
who tipped his hat and told me he much
preferred to be called Robert. Pshaw,

she said, You know I can see through you.
People raised on survival, I whispered.
Yes, yes, she breathed, You're seeing

differently. He accepts you for whoever
you aren't. He used to live in a '69
Cadillac. He believes in setting thighs on

fire, thinks he sounds more meaningful
when he screams. He is a circle you call
your self. I left thinking I am the whole

package at the wrong address, and I'm
too bored to run. The Void always sends
me to voicemail. That afternoon, under

a big sky, I discovered the Stargazer Lily,
whose petals urge toward heaven,
so I will call myself a Local Legend

and walk through the rain in a soft forest
of despair, insides floating into cloud
until my body is carried away by owls.

A Breath, Holding

In bed, after, you whispered, *This summer I want*
everything, and down the hallway I went in a

hotel robe fetching ice from the machine. Would
you say I'm a modern saint? Drunk a warmth,

not a weakness? The distance you covered since
last week when you were someone in a bar who

kept dancing to make it okay, even in the parking
lot where I lured you in my car with a blunt and a

pint, ruthless and gentle, lips pressing the back
of your neck, even in the soft belly of my half-

undressed tendency, how you do love me without
knowing me, without a care, with how little is

left of our pressing weakness, our towels dropped
in front of windows, the real happiness of no

questions or intentions, eating under the covers,
where it's later than you realize, although time is

just a big hit, a deep drag, a holding of breath,
holding, holding, and then the slow, sultry exhale.

My Opening Appearance

I read this poem for an exhibit opening in a local gallery.
Nobody knew what I was talking about, but they smiled kindly

and clapped when I signaled the end of the poem by smirking.
A young woman wearing a red shawl over her black hair

introduced herself after I'd finished reading and asked,
Would I read at the opening of her solo show? I said I would

if I could decipher what I was talking about. She said,
You may proceed. Outside, a bunch of skateboard punks

broke bottles, threw punches, and cheered in the parking lot.
A drunk photographer bought me a beer and explained in detail

her true passion was constructing miniatures, exact scale replicas
of abandoned places—gas stations and diners up and down

Route 66. It struck me that I didn't remember anyone's name,
that I couldn't name what my poem was supposed to be about.

This leather-jacketed, faux beatnik snapped his fingers and said
I had the rhythms right. He knows, he was there… Kerouac's

spectacular vernacular, Ginsberg's interlacing ecstasies.
How would I know what I should know about whatever it is

I'm talking about, I asked, but the gallery was empty and
the lights were out. Everyone had gone home to finish drinking.

I was standing in a dark space, hearing echoes, and had only
poems where the answers to my questions might have been.

*Last couplet inspired by Chase Twitchell.

Racing to the End

The electric company laughed
as we passed the last living trees,

barn rooves sloped away
into a tilted summer dark.

The future ended up lasting weeks and weeks—

we used it sparingly.

They had us arrested for trespass
with unremarkable faces, and yes, of course

we were drunk, with a few girls, shouting,
for blocks and blocks and blocks in our cars,

but other people sleep through their pain,
so why shouldn't we?

For us, the old bard sonnets pressed
too hard upon our feeble skulls

with the word *honor*— no such animal exists,
only the grief of angry gods,

and they should accept their deaths
just like the rest of us.

Art Made from Happiness Is Shit

There's a poem out there somewhere that begins
"When I look in a mirror, I see myself seeing myself."
So that's where we start: I dreamed I made a movie
about my imaginary Japanese girlfriend. Later,

in the hotel, she kept me up all night as a delightful
poem. Sure, the food was expensive. And I didn't
shower for days. Something was lurking in the obvious
fiction of the obvious danger I wanted to marry.

One morning she hopped out of bed and put on this
flirty skirt, nipple pink of course, as a dream would
make it in a head like mine, and I remember thinking
I should be lonely, but I'm not. I'm sitting in an

expensive decorative chair in a Bev Hills hotel room
naked and alive and willing to follow this middle-
school-feeling relationship anywhere. Afterlife
occurred as a possibility to me, also just plain

faking it, perhaps a paucity of imagination. Still,
she was happily some part of my personality, and I
was attracted to her in a pleasantly desperate way.
She let me try on her clothes. She dyed her hair

blue then red then green then blue again. I laid
for hours on my belly, nestled in the warm covers,
head propped in my hands, and watched her whirl
backwards asking, "How shall I wear my identity?"

Notes on the Transitory Nature of Things

The valley groves are gone and Coop still lives there.
There are purple and blue wildflowers in a field

behind the bankrupt strip mall down the road a piece.
There are eucalyptus, thick with leaves, that surround

a broken-down stable, thick with noble ghosts of horses.
Mostly Coop looks from his porch, or a window, as

animals come out of hiding, after chainsaws, short-order
cooks, and the sun have set down: opossum, stray dog,

a bobcat drifted far from its foothill. Coop has heard
neighborhood houses clearing—moving van, drunken

quarrel, gunshot, cursing and sobbing. Once he spotted a
mountain lion and a bear cub on a moonlit stroll down

his street, unlikely allies in a world of hunger. What was
Coop hungry for? his wife once asked him. He in turn

asked the toolshed, the kitchen floor, the counters at the
hardware store, but never received reply. Maybe he'll go

hiking. Lock the old place up and throw away the bills.
Maybe home looks like a fox and a deer... maybe

a wood and a highway. Maybe Robert Frost's grave.

I'll Ask to Walk Her Home

Mona Lisa's debut was actually a drag. Matisse arrived
from the future, on horseback, and fell right to sleep,

scissors in hand. The police brought Pete Rose up close.
He was in handcuffs, nose nearly pressed against her,

but soon he too was snoring, as the future tends to feature
better lighting and sound effects. Me, I went to school,

and there they told me her smile was everything about
western civilization captured in one slight, wry crease.

Her face will not, does not illuminate. And she cannot
play piano, as it hasn't yet been invented, which annoys

Wolfgang to no end. *I'll be whatever you want*, she says.
I can hear her— though Jesus and the Phoenix seem deaf.

Traffic signals are always yellow at the intersections
in my neighborhood, and I see her visage hanging in cool

morning colors. She says, *I left Leonardo behind a long
time ago.* I lay daises in the crosswalk. Want to drive her

in my '87 F-150 to the Sacramento River, sit and watch
a sunset. Want to build her an adobe house in the Mojave

Desert, far away from Joshua Tree, and walk her home.
I want to be the cure. Whatever she wants, I'll be that.

L.A. Three Ways

Behind

I woke at Hollywood Park, in bed, gardening, ten years past apocalypse to the day. To the hour. Traces of ruin still on her petals and leaves. We left through the pool. She trailed behind, rubbing glances with other men, actors or gamblers I swore, me sunburned to bust bright colors out their faces, fist against humping, donkey-face piñatas. I made only pop music. Reaching back for fingertips. To pull her forward— the song you hate to love and sing along whenever it sways out a rental car radio. Like I'd never felt fire in her hand. Skinny legs in skimpy bikini panning across palm trees and water and inexhaustibly hungry desert eyes. I begged her not to bloom under daylight. She left footprints in wet concrete. I slept on the ride back in Bunker Hill blues.

Beside

I meet a woman on Olympic Boulevard. Says she sees through secrets. The secret is she wants me dead. I have nothing else to do, so decide Sure—what the hell, and be over with quickly. No blood, but sirens, blue-red lights. On the ambulance ride, I try hard to make this Zen moment. But too late. I'm all teeth and claws predator, executioner in love. Too late. The rush is gone, and I sit up dead, imagining why a corpse would want to testify in court. I want my fantasy lover back. Death, ice-tray blue, secrets all bleeding. I want to need a woman who says nothing, sees even less.

Before

I will have everything you could ever want: bling-ka-ching! I will keep every catastrophe straight in my head. To forget will not be an option, nor will belief in tragic confirmation. To forgive will not even register, nor will tendency to comic anxiety. I will till and sow and bring freeway desert showers. Harvest oasis. Lie down in a burned out promise casino. Let the joy of a day just like the next glance over me, your fingers trailing down to rub and skinny one end-all, fuck-all disaster, single red and pistil blue plume giant against a grinding white smog staccato of sky, costume flying off, flesh curled in light, angel's flight vibrant illusion of water shimmering beneath ceaseless flutter of rain shadow. Shadows concrete, asleep, snoring through terror in L.A.

The Fall Approaches

He pressed his feet solid against the ground, alone,
a man, he thought, in the making. Present is best,

it's best to stay there, burrowed in "I exist," as the
empty thunders and rains wash the fiery roses and

sun strokes boil it down to malady. There's a rare
place of tonics to be found: moon over shoreline,

campfire, arms raised to blue-violet heavens, and
barber shops, dive bars, parking lots as big as lakes.

Who now from his grandfather's time. From what
barn or office building. Who will save his neck.

Who will chalk the cue, clear the table, and re-rack.
Whether bonding or shooting: Ideas of God. Needs

to embody a path, walk upright, walk righteous,
his father at the kitchen table with a bottle, his

mother in a car racing away. Summer tense, sharp,
iridescent, wholly ignorant of its imminent death.

II. We don't know any more than a dog
who watches the moon

High School Project

Jesus, yes, I slept on a mattress on the floor,
listening to ELP albums on headphones and

four-way window pane. And hell yes, after
I quit the team the football players called out

"Faggot!" from their passing cars. I drove my
shitty Nova from party to party searching for

an art class girl, interested in anyone who
was even slightly interested in me. Nobody

could see below the scars. My romantic, half-
closed hands, my eyes drawing complications

together, scratched Hendrix records and this
smashed heart my every weekend inheritance.

I was an alarm clock, an angry bear, and I
didn't mind. Dying locusts swarmed around

my eyes. Ask me if I lowered my chin (I did
not). Ask me if the hands of time kept asking

me to tough it out (they fucking did). I got a
check in the mail one day, borrowed a friend's

guitar, set the alarm clock on the windowsill
and sang, "Is it even in you, to love anyone?"

The Five Fires

She says, "Grimes makes me feel like I'm 15 again,
crying in an American Apparel dressing room."

She says she used to slump in her car before work,
listen to *Oblivion* and gradually accept her fate.

Hey, Lexie, if you didn't matter, you wouldn't be
telling me this. I was drunk yesterday

but somehow managed to online order two hoodies
and a 15th anniversary Blu-ray edition

of *Buffalo '66*. I ask her, Do celebrities have to be
famous on weekends? I'm thinking yes.

Let's give each other fat lips and hickeys.
Let's outgrow our appetite for mirrors and noise.

Tonight, in a January surrounded by five wild
fires and a desert, it's a supermoon so bright

the fenceposts can see their own loneliness, so get
ready to have your mind blown

by someone tired of always being so goddam right.
Energy, syzygy— you don't have to choose,

Lexie, because that's the way
we're doing things now: gas station bathroom selfies.

It had taken two years, the last two

of my father's life,
to get his lifelong childhood friend
to drive up from L.A.
and visit the Alzheimer's Happy Lodge
of No Return.
                    I just can't think of him
that way, Charlie would tell me on the phone,
so I just know I can't see it
up close.
            Why I
persisted in asking him I do not know,
but persist I did.

The morning he and his wife,
Barb, met me in front of Desert Garden
Memory Care Senior Living
the sun was shining,
                        the month was May, birds
flittering and chirping through trees walling
the multi-section building
                        and its advertised garden.
We greeted as if we hadn't met in ten years
because we hadn't.
                    We went inside and walked past
21-B, formerly
my father's room, and we walked through
the alarmed double-doors,
                        through the Lounge
of the Living Dead, a dozen or so vacant souls
staring through the TV
                    and into vast versions of nothingness,
with the occasional vague
                    fleck of regretful resentment,
and when the day nurse approached us
down the hallway to say

I'm so sorry, but
    your father passed away
        not five minutes ago,
Charlie and his wife stopped mute, maybe relieved.

I kept stride and went directly
inside the door of a room my father had been
hidden in
        to writhe through
the last agonizing weeks of his hard-earned
        lonesome and loathsome life,

and I saw pillowed there
the last anguish suspended on his face and cried
What have you done now
            you stupid old man,
what have you done…
                you always got everything wrong
                    god-dammit,
and Lo, I could hear my voice as if someone else
were wailing above the gruff of blackbirds
while I felt only
        that I could let it go—
                    The Hatred,
knowing nothing
            but that I was talking to myself,
that the mask of his face
                would haunt me,
that now he was waiting for me
under a tree of forgotten pity.

White Coyote

Coyote, sandbaggers drove you off the back nine today.
I saw you slicing low under sugar-pine boughs, across
concrete and into a flood pipe.

I heard you later, bark whistling between your missing teeth
as you crashed the country club's Mexican buffet.

Coyote, roadhogs ran you off the parkway at half-past noon.
I saw you skittering around nervous Dodges, across
pavement and into a mud ditch.

Coyote, years ago you saw crows pluck out both my eyeballs.
You heard me shouting seven days for your help, across
rivers and into the rich muck.

I hear your gush tonight through my open window, yowling
about mercy, incessantly, in the yellow moonlight.

Coyote, you stare up at me with primordial blue orbs.
You watch me leap-dog onto my wooden dresser, across
bedsheets and into a dark hall.

Coyote, you see me startle and make for an open door.
I spring and bolt for the fence-gate to give you chase, over
dry sagebrush and into an arroyo.

I smell the piss of wilderness on your coat. Miles off, instinct
says to raid a campsite, summoned by its lurid flame—

Coyote, you wheel and race into night's blind beauty, vanish
behind night's smoke, fire I'll finally steal for myself.

Osculation

On the radio I hear about this restaurant, Kali's Lips, and we sit around a table that's got a wonky leg. I say *"Mua,"* to the cute Indian waitress with the scarred cheek, blowing a kiss as she takes the order. You surprise with whiskey, rice, coconut, hilsa with lentils, talk of migratory hearts. I watch and catch a gold anklet dance with *Mua's* bare feet, soft back to the kitchen steam. Already, you say, you hear fish circling in a brown pond. Already, you say, there are cormorant hisses, snow furrowing pond's edge. An apron-looking woman peeks from a table behind, orange freckles, buttery mouth, and her eyes purse—I want to fall, buoyant. You begin to hum. Start to slide ribs out from under your skin, pile bones on the cloth next to the centerpiece vase, the droopy, drying orchid. Tender. Careful. I try to remain optimistic. Your chest sags, withers, wrinkles. *Mua* reappears, one dark knee lifted beneath orange sari, our amber-gold glasses and warm oval plates floating down her four arms to rest before us. I see a knife in her hand, a glint, a few seconds of blood, then your heart pulsing beneath the cage of her fingers. "Listen," she whispers. Whiskey licks at the rim. Rice holds itself in. Coconut floats in snow leopard milk. And hiding in lentil shoals, little fishes spin mouth to tail, and this is an answer, I think, but not from your pulse in her delicate palm. This is the zero before and the zero after. This is water. The oscillation of Love, and is shaped like water. Again I see the wife behind you, and from a tiny corner of her look she begs, "Do not pull yourself from unruly green sea—don't be fooled by dry land," airborne kisses lapping at the turn of my cheek.

Lost Letter to Emily

Everyone here is drinking beer, big whooping clouds
passing over, Mojave sun microwaving us all, everything
hot to the touch, so the beer gets warm fast, meaning

Jimmie & Vero & all that crowd are gulping Modelos,
letting out circus-tent laughs on the picnic grass here by
the stables. I'm keenly watching horses stroll, mostly, or

yipping when I stroke their necks. Last night Jimmie's
sister, Tina, found me on the back porch of my little faux-
adobe duplex & full-on kissed my stray mouth. I have

missed her & it was a gift. I've missed you, too, but
differently, like a ghost limb. Tina split this morning with
ass-hat photographer you-know-who. No surprise, that.

Remember him hitting on you, after your broken ankle
bareback riding the Narrows? He's still got the scar—
man, I was proud of you. I am now quitted on the warm

beers & have started on a bottle of bourbon. Yes, the
Heaven Hill Green. Yes, still having that same dream:
summer in San Gabriel Valley orange groves, scooting

around on the banana seat of my Schwinn Sting-Ray,
& Jesus steps out from behind a tree to say, That, right
there, that's the poem, right now, in your mongrel head!

Elegy with First Love Regret in It

Come on, you said, *You know what I mean.*
Kindness. Later that night
I dreamed in a deer's silence about

the cabin, the snowstorm, the fire
beside which Jenny kiss'd me. Beauty.
My dream jump-cut to summer, origami,

abortion, Memphis, car lights shining on
motel windows. Does that
answer your curiosity? The icy twigs of

your black question. Because each memory
is a book in itself, and lined up
on a shelf they scarcely suggest a life.

I missed her. I lost her. I didn't get it
back then, Jenny moving like
a cloud through sky moving through water.

Come on, you say, *You knew about lies,*
forgiveness, finishing
each other's dangerous thoughts…

yes, and walking through afternoons, dumb
with balloon-like buoyancy
on the street. Rain, mud, death's weight.

What I'm trying now to say—
I'm trying to say we are all human.
So I'm trying hard to smile when I say it.

She Was Clean Until the Night She Died

Someone asked me were her eyes crazy as her poems. Yes,
I said, Glazed like graffitied metal trash bins in the sun,

spilling over with secondhand treasure. Beneath the worn
leather jacket, a floral print dress floated around her,

and she was pure money—human bliss currency, intricate
sci-fi tattoos the length of both arms, a Burroughs girl,

distress and desire and a yes no yes to the universe, pain in
pleasure, pleasure in pain, her darkness the creator

of light. She could improvise, read aloud from a phonebook
back then and make *Howl* sound like nursery rhyme.

If she went to bed with you, you were lost, a damn junkie,
a walking, talking craving willing to do anything

for the smallest part in her smallest satisfaction. She was
always in a fix she didn't want to get out of, promises

clean, tangled head tilted back to Patti Smith's *Horses...*
whatever you want to know about her, it won't be enough.

Undressed

I dreamed we started making love again, that we
slept deeply, waking refreshed, remembering our
dreams. There were orange butterflies in a garden
we planted together, wing dust floating like fine
galaxies. Warblers sang, sparrows chittered, then
I looked back to see your face… you were crying
Algean tears, smile wrenched to grim. The birds
dispersed and night fell with a thud, like a thick
black velvet curtain. I was alone in bed, again.
That you were never happy. A callused love that
grew through me like a Puncture Vine, a single
star-shaped violet flower each spring, sticky with
truth: *you were never happy.* That when I remove
my old clothes, I am a colorless shade of naked.

Ghost Chasing

As if I am a boy again, the moon following me
everywhere, like light reflected in my mother's

green eyes, or the still surface of Silverwood Lake
at midnight. "No one alive is alone," according

to Helen, perpetually upbeat, but her opinion
counts less because she is so much prettier than

the rest of us. Still, she has a point. I've lived in
Alaska's birch cathedrals, late of the great state

of Americans trying to escape their damn selves,
but guess what... people already live there, and

runaways are just toting their problems around
to pin on unsuspecting souls. I've tried to run

away from you, too, but of course give in. I keep
a photo of you in my wallet— your beaming

face right after I kissed you. Your death is a
perplexing beauty: this welcome obligation to

cinematic memory, emotional mythos, flights of
stairs in my sleep that lead through lusty shadow

or flowery grief, nights slightly longer, mirrorless
halls full of doors randomly locked or unlocked,

rooms empty of ghosts, although I feel the delicate
warmth of wood fire from some chamber or other,

catch feints of ember and ash, so I search on,
resolute, calm, moon watching through a window.

Poem Ending with a Line from Luc Besson's "Lucy"

Dad treasured Anne Murray's *Snowbird*, like to wore that record out until, during a case of Coors with a neighbor, he heard the double whammy: he'd been listening to a Canadian lesbian. He broke what he loved, threw it out. I wear jeans & a sportscoat to the service, no tie, pay the choir to sing *Snowbird*. My sister paints her nails during my eulogy. After, back at the house, store-bought potato salad, deli platter, neighbors & relatives chatter on anything but Dad, who hated hard, though me & Sis do not, us both excommunicated for relations with gays & not-whites, despite his Mexican buddy & drunk holiday habit of dancing around singing in one of Mom's dresses "as a joke." Always kept a dog to kick, yell at, lock outside at night, & muttered dark evangelical passages, trapped between the fool's gold of heaven & his seething lust. Sis thinks she had him figured. I did too, for a time, us both kicked & locked out of home, but I've thought more about it since, parked by the river, under the cottonwood at night—truth is, we don't know any more than a dog who watches the moon.

Northbound Mojave Highway

There are only so many stories in all the world,
and they are all the same.
                              In this story,
there is a long-dead woman,
                              grief-stricken. In this story,
there is a son obsessed
with a father's death.

          Any evidence that can be recorded
          has equal significance:

the father as a young tough, his leather jacket,
                              and here are the names
of the Corona High School girls
who watched him, of the long-dead Rosemead girl
                              who touched him,
and see here those
          doo-wop song lyrics they all sang to
on the car radio,
those naive lines flowing
          into all of his love letter sentences,
followed by the unintended marriage license,
          the unwanted birth certificates.

The long-dead woman he used to write to
bursts into tears,
desert rain, into which her son floods and steers.

Dear Mother, Do You Recall

I was ten years old, and drew a meaningful picture for you,
a dream of you becoming me. One day only, but enough to
float above the swimming pool your husband paid for instead
of the air conditioning you'd begged for, for years. In the
picture, Rusty was loose in the backyard barking at contractors
and biting your husband's feet, which were bare and well-
traveled, pedicured by other ladies. You see his naked soul:
a trembling sparrow, with piranha teeth. You see future me
learning to sing amphetamine-and-pearl-spattered Dylan songs
until they tattoo my brain. You see through my pupils as my
mind is consumed with glossy hair, soft curves, easy smiles,
mosquito kisses. Gasping marriage. You hear through my
drums the sparrows coming home to my yard, by the hundreds.
All garbles and whispers, my singing voice gone to gravel.
You touch with my fingers, reaching to strangle the dank
creature in the mirror. You feel my neurotransmitters. You
become my desperate pity and love for you, in this long sleep.

Sand, Stone, and Ash

Dawn highlights verdigris on the brass Lion's Head gate
as shadows begin to stretch across lawn's dirty headstones,
wave of stratus clouds swishing in from the coast. I bruise
here easily. Don't want to unlock, unloose you, but we're
captive audiences, you and I, mirrors and jokes, so I come
for the bronze air instead of a howling moonlight. Your
eyes closed to wait for death. Underground, strolling hills
in a breeze, you've become closer as a stranger, even more
talkative, arms stretched-out, eyes still closed while deer
and rabbit graze around you. The L.A. skyline floats on.
I wish the ocean would salt-wash my ears and tongue,
render me raspy and deaf, and I'll forgive you again, later,
over a whisky, without tears or hesitation, even as the black
velvet ice of stars lays upon me, even as you've gone to
placid sea, no fear or punishment, flat and shiny as glass.

Here

I do experience loss, a sense of one's own illness,
and I don't like idle talk or being judged. Probably

I've visited her twenty times. I didn't want to be
invisible in California, or sadly surprised, so she

taught me a different way of working, challenged
play to become something more. Look, this is just

fucking madness here, Ted Kaczynski not a disease
but a symptom and all they do is blame Islam now

because Scientology, Marilyn, and Rock 'n Roll ain't
workin' anymore. You only need to take a cab in L.A.

to understand the many intersections here, straight
white men trying to steer through HIV, assault rifles,

Tijuana, Big Pharma, Black America, Hollywood
playgrounds, Playboy sans nudity, Red Lobster,

bankruptcy, hecklers, open questions about Queer.
I'm here, lodged between the Airport Hilton and

homemade fear, and she's driving down to save me.
I've given her nothing, deserve nothing. *Imagine*

dragging yourself, she said on the phone last night,
So then you'd get to decide where to be pulled…

pre-9/11 simplicity, pre-Katrina NOLA, anytime
anywhere pre-Internet…

I said no, none of those. Maybe something in a new
comic book hero, with a noir passion for isolation,

a future-sick sense of here, now, of one's own loss.

Trick or Treat

Isn't it always ending, the world, its sweet spots,
she says, passing behind me in the mirror, *Like a*
bowl of fruit on a table, pomegranates maybe, left
in the sun, rotting because they're so full of light.

Does loneliness have a date of expiration? Buddha
would need anti-depressants if he lived here, now.
I've been reading Larry Levis, again, for two weeks
straight. She meditates daily, on a rug beneath this

painting—an F.D.R. era triptych: destitute workers
building a bridge under an orange San Francisco sky,
migrant Central Valley pickers, L.A. cops beating
a young black man with billy-clubs like a mule off

its farm. Same sweet sun lights up every mischief,
eats every person, place, and thing in its radius—
once it tires of us, it'll collapse in its own glimmer,
like that jack-o-lantern you left out on your porch.

Holy War

Can't feel my feet in the fire, can't afford a drink in heaven.

A hundred ways to drive down
      the mountain without snow tires.

Deer and a salt lick and a tree felled on a wet road
my father haunted with his shotgun and a hat.

There ought to be a clear cut exit through these trees—

      ought to be a law against acts committed
by a man on a Mission from God.

Somewhere, right now, that man has his finger on a trigger.

Politic

Faced with being nailed to a cross, sure, you'll bring
the money tomorrow—I'm in the wrong, you'll say,
I'm not even listening, will come the reply, but
you aren't listening, instead fixated on the sound
of a hammering future. Is love inconstant?
Kill him with his own gun. Is joy inconceivable?
Hang all hope from the scaffold. What kind of
opinion does the sun have, or a mutt, or some small
gathering of birds on a wire. You will pay your debt
with a chainsaw if you can get away with it.
You will keep your blade sharp. Pointless arguments
drift off, serene clouds of unreachable compromise,
as the grind of human supplication and mercilessness
sustains this unremitting tremble in the poisoned air.

Another Victor Valley Summer

Freaking hot, so what's new in the
desiccated view, my head sopped like
a filthy mop, and all I see is trucks, all
these trucks, why so many goddam

trucks and Call of Duty losers who
pay to wash them every day! When I
had my F-150 (R.I.P.), rain washed it
or I hosed it off in my driveway, me

sucking on a beer bottle like dark art.
Any way we look at truth it creaks,
then protest like Jeanine, who's always
fogged, or worse—wired, with thirty

milligrams of Ritalin kicking in plus
three and a half grams of homegrown
shrooms, but, really, she's a kind of
masterpiece, coming up your gravel

driveway, opening your gate, glaring
through your front window, so if you
leave the porchlight on she'll be there:
wiping her eyes, claiming to be clean,

no privacy, half-naked interloper, an
unwashed truth right before you. Can
you bring yourself to dance with it, or
would you stare like it's on a screen,

a movie character you'll study, later,
if you have the time, as decades pass
with Jeanine's mascara still smeared,
and we inch through the day, back to

our bedrooms, our mosquito dreams,
distant laments, strange and precious.

Suicide Notes Left for Los Angeles—No. 1

L.A. River a falsehood, drug-induced concrete arroyo, a bleak grandeur which humiliates my similarly rigid solo, stanza by stanza claiming the city, insanity. Wanda long gone, Bukowski a situation and not a mere man, Luis Rodriguez tall along with Natalie Diaz, J.P. Dancing Bear and other struggles, tribes and clubs and guns. Do your work. Sentiment is agriculture, said Farmer Synecdoche of the laboring hands, rough, muscular, pulling a chair up to the table for you to sit. Immigrants, yes, *All language is spiritual here!* says the voice inside my typewriter. Hypocrisy a bus ticket and a last kiss on the cheek. California refineries tower as gambling houses charm, redwood park benches are shaped to fit fat asses. Let's remember the Central Valley and the Navy. Two Chinatowns. Mexico's hot breath in our hair. It's clear, no, emphatic: bored lovers on Xanax, medical weed, expense account. Where hotels plead for sleep while the bar is always open. Brassy pawned saxophones making love to snob pianos, the slightest smile returned by a knowing glance. Lights dim, a little smoke. No one here is checking the time. Perilous as an indoor swimming pool, days accidental, Los Angeles has stopped trying to be a Mark Jarman poem.

Suicide Notes Left for Los Angeles—No. 2

In school I had friends whose parents let Indian peacocks roam their back yards. Another passing California phase, piercing calls, green-eyed plumage fanned atop wooden suburban fences. Lawns fawned over by alcoholic fathers. No angels perched in our palm trees. It was later, at some beach or other—Huntington, Laguna, Redondo maybe, where lost spirits cluster in shorts and bikinis and sandy hats—that I called it what it was: black witchcraft. A Pacific sunset view opposed by stinking, mindlessly bobbing urban oil well pumps. Good looking people saying and doing terrible things. Neon blinking behind smog or fog, depending on time of day. Civilization was a movie theater. Assembled representation. Be seated: these are buttered popcorn anecdotes and drive-thru scenes, collaged by strangers somehow lonelier than yourself. Don't hold still, I say, not for Elvis or Marilyn or compositions of color so beguiling you cry for hours remembering your childhood. Time to de-contextualize, a hundred junkies for every church. Dexter Gordon in the wee hours bouncing notes off of dead whiskey bottles. Bebop a belonging. Bumming a smoke. Passing a joint. Gloom and ghetto and glamour our muses.

Suicide Notes Left for Los Angeles—No. 3

Catch a cab at the airport, give the Lebanese driver the Santa Monica address. I, poor pilgrim of sorrow, like an unemployed Richard Gere, have nowhere else to go. Night hovers cold over desert to the east. When it collapses into the L.A. River, ambling at the coast, climbing though windows in suburban valleys, it means to conceal. Her apartment door is tagged Spanish red and green, knob newly replaced, complemented with a fist-sized hole. Tawny plants sag in little pots by the stair rails. Night runs straight to the door when it opens, and a sweet hashish fog rolls around her finely glazed face. I follow her silhouette. Like Dennis Hopper's ghost, I've played every fair in this part of the country. The floor laughs, low, delirious, as I boot empty beer bottles in the living room. Groggy gray figures speckle sofa and chairs along the way. Wall sockets sigh. Light bulbs drowse, fulvous, dream of flying everywhere at once, like a pale memory of sunlight. Red-eyed kitchen table caterpillars, worming in haze, pass a pipe, and I drag long, faze into a zone once left behind, where I find an old self, not waving but frowning, who shivers in the heart of his late scrim day.

Backyard Beers & Thoughts with Two Jocular Dogs

The comic bark of a neighbor's dog is none of my beeswax.
The mad grass slapping in the wind, the stubborn petals

grasping their stem, the gas station meth-mouthed prophets,
the Q-Nuts and their squash-soup-colored acolytes, these

are all sawdust left on the workshop floor of Creation. So, too,
the swimming pool sky, a hawk that circles the bronze sun,

those plushie clouds ambling the globe like Bardo hobos.
The mystery of folded hands. Of hair and breasts and warm feet.

Of kisses and cocks and pussies, of babies and shit and long,
luxurious pees. The wonders of cancer and kuru. Of work.

Of disability and unemployment and social security.
Of poverty. Of charity. All this workshop detritus, this is my

business, my enterprise, to surmise from a bourbon-dark pool
of stagnant water some formula for prayer, some litany

for listening, some PVC, duct tape, and beer can construction
of eloquence that will make me want to wake, come morning.

A cat crosses my yard, warily, disguised as a soul. My Aussie
wags her stubby tail, barks poetic her risible canine code.

Poem Ending with a Line by Frank O'Hara

I am listening to a jazz record in this tiny room,
                                        a love song,
reading a little book, *Meditations in an Emergency*,
sipping a very fine old bourbon because
Frank O'Hara is the consummate American
                    of a now dead story named "America."

Thank the cold harvest of stars
he is not alive to see what happens outside these walls.
Movies gone to pot, urbanity siphoned off
                                into papier-mâché
            of secondhand despots,
propped up on television with marionette mouths.
        What utterances are these?

Someone's hired
                a band of chimpanzees to interpret;
meanwhile, *Body and Soul* fills our room.
        What Miró-like longing is this? remembering
                Maribel the summer
                                I owned the known world.

She could, oh yes, magnificently and then some,
so calm made of pure fire,
                    kisses lounging between us, me emptied
like a pail of dirty water watching her walk away,
a tease of wind
            in her skirt of red and green—
                                what days,
and what did I have to live for but her attention,
wisps of black curl wild near her soft brown ear.

Intelligence
            has had nothing to do with itself
            in our century.
I am a fool for art's sake and keep company likewise.
Frank knows what I mean when he says,
"men cry from the grave while they still live."

III. Counterweight to a vast, sad, damned world

Diminishment

I am addicted to the sound of water.
I don't need to tell you that drowning is impossible for a poem.

I'm not compelled to be this transparent or well-intentioned.
I can lift all things, carry them along.

I understand you will hang and burn me in Photoshop'd effigy.
The diminishment of culture is unavoidable.

I'm not married to the idea of progress.
I don't need to describe the beer or the threadbare relationships.

I'm not elevated or vain or nuts.
I understand that some of you are tender and good and whole.

The diminishment of rain is a slow curl of dove-colored smoke.
I am addicted to the sound of water.

The Reading

I walk into the small bookstore on a violet-black
desert summer evening, strands of twinkling white
light reflected in the plate glass, pachouli oil and a
whisper of high-grade weed sweetening the air.

I slip into a back-row folding chair, while you hold
your new book like a sacred text and read to the
audience an imaginary letter to an old lover, and it
takes a minute, a few details, but at last I recognize

myself in those lines, can feel the breath of them on
my neck, in Barstow, afternoon, 1989, rustling
sheets in a motel, TV on to muffle little screams.
You were full bloom on the life and death edge of

your marriage. I was young and overflowed with
premature smoke, giddy sex, always-too-soon-a-
feeling… didn't understand impossible then. You
in your warm bath, bright and witty, keeping our

bodies humid and intertwined. But tonight, you are
full of corpses. Reading from a book of the dead.
There will be no resurrections, only a bitter mist
of metaphors, we two trapped in the backseat of a

taxi that's been released from gravity and careens
into a deep, cold, silent space….

The Other Side of Night

Mother getting there first, then my father, my little sister.
The dead, as the line goes, keep dying, and by brutal

increments of lost. Even photographs seem foreign
correspondence, eventually. Whether they leave by angles

or angels, life is a dream three times a day: waking,
dissolving into R.E.M.s, the feathery drifting in between.

My sister and I are still black-winged confederates, the night
still divorcing us from our parents. We always end up in

the high trees, pearly-toothed constellations and a low moon
casting long-leaved shadows below, fire smoking nearby,

droning planes of recently deceased passing overhead.
We don't much need to speak, my sister and I, knowing what

we do about things, like about the canopy's waver,
the never-explicated hint of daybreak. We are together apart.

Mom per usual has made dark friends amid the wood,
wounded deer and famished wolf and dumbfounded bear.

Dad just stares and frowns at his isolation in eternity,
all the while sitting on a slunk branch, right next to me.

Every Map Leads to Catastrophe

— after Eduardo C. Corral

Catastrophe is a blown tire, a ruptured eardrum.
With the first sneeze, catastrophe spreads madly.
Catastrophe clutches us like cuffs of wolf spider.
We cannot ignite catastrophes as we do laser beams.
In some musical theories, catastrophe is a perfect pitch.
Earflap caps warm the icy mind of catastrophe.
Like Kama Sutra, catastrophe will screw you 64 ways to Sunday.
Catastrophe walks its dog off-leash, proud of its bite.
Federal law requires you wear your catastrophe anklet.
Happiness smuggles catastrophe in a lonesome coat.
In my hands, catastrophe flowers like ragweed.
Catastrophe is best served in a spicy love gumbo.
Atop my hut of catastrophe, a million pigeons shit.

Forgive me, Father, for I

who have prayed, pray so little
anymore, in the old way. I hold the words
in the cloister of my mouth,
smother them in soft folds
of thought, suffocate their
coming to the tongue. The old words…

our Father who art, hallowed be
these eggs and toast, forgive my lust,
banish greed and give me rest
each day, each night, these fifty-six years.

I listened well as a child,
Father, waking to kneel in musty rooms,
doors left cracked, sometimes
kneeling outdoors under ravens and
cardinals, matins rising with birdsong to
gather among eucalyptus leaves.

The trees are different here. Here,
I am changed. Sliding through calmer
summers, bracing against
onslaughts of spring wind…

I have come, of late, grown weary of
shrillness, aching for ease, out to the old
groves, where I might hear the hum
when light breaks over the spired branches.

Feeble September

Under the fleece of sleep, starlight music is
spilling over me, and I follow her, room to room,
her laugh an out-of-tune piano, glimpses of her

golden phantom hair pulling me into worship.
By morning, life is a makeshift house, slippery
black rocks. A drunk dad, like everyone had.

The somber cello of mother. I ran the riverbed,
school a coiled staircase leading nowhere, but
in manic summer, blankets splayed by the lake,

covered with frenzied bodies, and midnight's
wet grass, laid on my back to lift my hands,
hold the moon. I've called her Grace, chased her

in forests and deserts and such strangely familiar
houses. I've almost seen her face a thousand times
but never quite. Now and then a smile or even

a flash of fair breast, she dashes through rooms,
or between trees, or glides into a star-riddled
August Mojave dark. By daylight, I mumble

to myself. Bloodied. Creak-boned. By night I ride
wings, explore orchards of temptation. On land,
memories baked into dry riverbed. Shadows

invite. I can hear her laugh. A sigh, as she peels
off the shoulder of her dress. I died decades ago,
Bible verses sprinkled over my corpse, feeble

September slipping to disconsolate winter,
where I moan for July, August, another sparkle
of green eyes, another sleeping beauty kiss.

Ending Up at Seven Grand for Drinks & Jazz

She says the history of her life is a chokepoint
in need of a firm plunge, & you're a cute sort of
possible infection, or maybe plague. She's not
sure yet. She removes her overcoat like great
heron wings, almost legendary, already everyone
in the place ogling— coyote smiles as she slides
into the booth, you just a witness & grateful for
your olfactory senses bathing naked in fragrance,
obsessed with how it will taste when you close
your eyes to kiss. Explore the shape of her tongue.
Two martinis please, very dirty, & then you think
remember to breathe: eyelashes, jade irises, her
fingers tickling your arm & a bird laugh, so it
makes no difference if her lips are razors, if she's
come to steal your car, leave you for dead on a
Wilshire Boulevard curb, since you're in for all
of it, the burns, cuts, abrasions, to swim, touch,
change all your colors in the virtuosity of night.

April and October

A strange bed.
Naked, curled around another
fresh start.
At 59, beginnings are cruel.
Like the air here
in this coastal motel.
Rooms full of bored ghosts who
can't be bothered
to haunt lovers anymore.

Dawn is blue with expired pleasure,
legs and arms
and gull shit
on the rickety balcony.

I pushed you
last night
to a certain will,
found you weak, muted city flesh—
soy milk,
hyper-white skinned,
silver turquoise native bracelets,
with just enough grass and speed
to keep a phantom firm.

Now
it's like a dry mouth, the day
unquenchable,
unforgiving.
Not enough vodka in the world
to keep
up with my disappointment.

I brought you
to this crummy little beach town

to search for you
among the RVs, the dumbfounded
families,
the stray dogs with enough intelligence
to run away from home.
But the coast
was sloughed with fog
as we curved around the ridge
listening on the radio
to one of my
stupid California love songs.

What you said,
in the parking lot
coming out of the Thai restaurant
weeks ago, was right.
What is wasn't ever,
is now triumphant in its defiance
of what we see
to think, hear to hold.

We've subsisted on a sadness
like cake Antoinette
until our weight pushed our wheels
flat to the ground,
baggage in the trunk
tumbled in the road,
our skewed headlights throwing
faint yellow fists
at a duplicitous mist,

as if the highway wanted a fight,
as if this specter would ever let us win.

Bliss Feels Like Shit

Isolated in the Mojave Motor Inn
after getting beat up by vegan tourists in Joshua Tree.
A couple of Lance Corporals
from Twentynine Palms Marine Corps base witnessed it
and told the lady cop they
would have intervened but for the glitter in their eyes
from tongue swapping in a
tent pitched at the National Park. They said they had
no idea who Gram Parsons was,
and just then a symbolic dog wandered by with that
I miss my junkyard look in its eye.
I'm left feeling ornery, homeless as an Amboy creosote,
strangely drawn to the mysterious
and scrappy lady cop, despite her ragged inventory.
She has spirit, and I'm on a quest.
What is loved? What is lost, irrevocably? What the hell
is the deal with primal desert
elements evoking existential dreamscapes? Oh, and
what exactly am I supposed to
gaze at silently for hours in these deep Mojave stellar
nights? I'm coming of age once again.
I want to haunt stillness, not these junkyards or wrecked
homes or alluvial desert canyons
where bodies are always buried. I think mystery is a
dynamic attractor: in this case,
a lady cop with dimensions beyond my homelessness.
I think we could be an animal mind,
she and I, fearless, sojourning through danger's kingdom.
This in the pit of night, which is
no small thing out in Joshua Tree, USA, where stars are
scattershot, as random as
human thoughts or bullets or inexplicably severe desires.

At Sixty, a Young Woman Can Be Mistaken for a Spiritual Experience

He thinks about life after death, decides not to believe—
once around is enough. Decides secretly to be a large
hibernating mammal waking up to call himself "B. Curious."

He stopped talking to Santa late (at eight), though Saint Nick
seemed realer than Holy J.C., who was really kind of a drag.
Nothing worse than a lecturing hippie. Television

did in a pinch. But now! Sleepy time is over. Mother died,
then he only had sister, and she died, too, so together
that makes Two Wolves and a Bear. Coyotes hang around

bungalows once occupied by contract actors. What sort of
paradise was that, one wonders, during those golden
reeling years. And what are poets thinking, anyway,

optimism always giving in to gravity because we need to
believe in the kind of everyday failing we do, as a matter
of course, obvious, and in need of a song. He wouldn't have

flapped homemade wings except for poets falling, too.
At this Hollywood bar and grill, he thinks you are glamorous.
He thinks you are in his price range. That you are either

mysterious or a case of buyer's remorse. Whichever way,
he's going to regret not regretting you. You're so beautiful,
he growls softly, How do you even have to pay rent

in this world. He sees right through you through Jeffrey
Lebowski shades. Outside, coyotes crowd The Strip
to watch you drive your new white Lexus right into the sun.

What Doesn't Love You

L.A. is all about idiolatry. No point in the specifics.
Perfect looks flash by like two a.m. sirens on Sunset.
Love, you ask? Love slips sensation back in your body

and ecstasy in your mouth, as you gawk a fabulous
B-Lister jaw about hunger and affluence. When you get
your big break, luck will let you forget love... won't

that be nice? Tell the truth, if you remember how:
isn't Los Angeles a name for knowing you arrived
with savage intentions? No amount of disappointment

can scrape you clean as you need to be. Life flirts be-
tween blue ambulance echoes, obscured by Hollywood
detachment. Or is it intimacy? Distinctions matter

less and less. Your favorite movie will end, its reels
spilling out the window, into the desert street. The sad
girl high above love on the ledge of the building

bends her legs and raises her arms to fly. You walk off
the set, wondering why America wants to kill you.

I wanted to be

that young woman
leaping from a tall building,
which I cannot do
because my body is made of sky
and to fall through myself
is what makes me a man,
this dying upward.

The Entrepreneur and His Fortunes

The difference between coincidence and fate
is a full kiss of self-replica, of correctible vision.

I made some horrible mistakes.
I'm not really suggesting anyone should be like me.
I had this wild Tarot experience.

The cards said, "True power lies in forbidden thought."

Rub a throbbing Rabbit on each other's buttocks
and tummies. Rather than shoot for the moon,
ride wave-like. Now think about the tides
you put between you and you.

Sail on, say the cards, get real, surrender to subservience—

on your knees while she stands in front of you.
She's grabbing my ears for navigation.
I'm lapping cream, sea-salty lips, safe, like in the back
of cop cars. Like a cup of coffee warms my hands.

An accident realized, I'm in an accidental business.
Captains and corporations serendipitously find

we're blind. You don't really know what people want,
until you start to do it.

Tom's Celebrity Cruise

You leave your pants in Venezuela,
a gift to some come-lately soap opera star.
Your Zen-waist trousers end up in a TV commercial
opposite an old girlfriend,
Serena, or Jaren maybe,
technically stretched between business and pleasure.
Your new girlfriend makes love because
there's no rapture for the wicked. Sundays you do it
on the rooftop, with a New York Times
and orange juice. It's a predilection for bi-polar barmaids
with Vegas showgirl cousins that drugs you—
mermaids singing through shark's teeth.
Tomorrow you'll board ship
for Costa Rica, luggage
lighter, colonialist prick a compass
to even saltier melody. The closer you get to the U.S.
the more you screw like a maniac fist.

We Cover Our Heads from Light

Hunched over women walk through town, homes
hitched to their backs. Random men
stand around, forgive themselves little by little, for fifty years.
Boys stain shirts, girls twirl toes, wondering where they'll fit in.

Everyone either a mule or a poet.
Everyone waits at night to wake in a different world.

Everybody awakes angry skin oiled in dreamy ferment.
Everybody awake drinking feigned disappointment.

A man on the corner of boy-stained streets
holds out lilies to a girl who spins to the ground.

Her stocking feet stick out from under the plank house.
Which witch? Everybody wants to know.
Everyone wishes a secret wish when her toes curl up to heaven.
Everyone wants it quick and painless, mostly based on television.

Hunched over our microwavable mac and cheese dinners,
we say to the sad girl on TV, "That's a beautiful hat."

In Bed with Time and Fire

These days I wake up in the feeling
of that lost drunk morning, camped at Yucca Valley
in the curious Roadrunner Motel,
neon cooled out after Lebanese Blonde constellations had

faded. Be not lustful, I repeated to myself
until the buzz under that dome of blue-red planets
leaned me ever closer while we hiked
between boulders and creosote, strange night collapsing

around us, June air fragrant
with sage and purple and soft orange light on your skin—
when restraint buried itself like a tortoise
under my humid heart. O the look of surprise, the horror

in your amethyst eyes when I bedded
a kiss on the flush pink of your unsuspecting mouth!
There was the awkward path back to the room,
the timorous music tuned-in on the post-war radio,

and soon affection poured out of a warm bottle,
copper-gold whiskey distilling the odd earlier moment,
then roiling laughter, laying us down
on a greedy bed, where those unutterable spells were cast.

Morning's heat spread open a hungover Sunday,
taboo lurking over our silence on the malignant drive back,
but now, unable to bait, trap, or lure
your conversation for lo these four plus decades since,

unwilling to flush you out cheaply
by metastasizing reports of my impending permanent sleep,
these days I awaken in that drunken bed
with our cruel sun, feathers scattered, pillows warm,

where I swear to these three sacred truths:
I was never supposed to need you, I have always loved you,
an unforgiving furnace of stars will have us yet together.

Inside Straight / Shot in the Dark

Bought a Prius when I retired, driving to Santa Rosa
to see her. Stopped at a Black Bear Diner: toast, bacon,
hashbrowns, eggs over easy. The wry waitress said,
Nice beard. In her apartment, Julie sat at a computer,

typed me an email that said, Unbutton my silk blouse.
Hocked her wedding ring to buy the PC. Back home in
Mojave, winds will blow from the south, northeasterly,
as coyote pups engage in a common play behavior

known as "hip-slam." One night, Julie drunk drove to
Needles from L.A. at ninety miles per hour. She found
devotion a joke and it was a nice time to die. Why
would anyone give up even one moment, I asked when

she told the story. She said, I'm going to live. Night
slopes in and sky is clouding fast as I flash northward
on the I-5, while somewhere a black bear is staring
at stars, chewing a deep bear thought. Julie stayed

in Needles, got a dog, married, made American cheese
sandwiches every afternoon, and I moved to Alaska
to start over. Rain avalanches everyone on the road—
I wait two hours for a jack-knifed semi to be cleared.

Julie keeps drinking coffee, texts about her fave
Megadeth songs and her fear of breast cancer. I text
images of birds. She got into poker, Omaha Hi-Lo,
and last Saturday explained all the rules to me. Music

is enough to sustain my will to live. Car window fogs
and it's hard to see in this torrent but what I know is
a sign will appear if I keep driving, so I go on, with
Beethoven's less-heroic sixth swimming in my head.

Scruff

She acquainted him with the sleepless
solitude of unquietness. A black bear
crept into the tent of their nights together
and ate the sunrise. Instead of the flower
that led him into bed, his nostrils flared with
wet fur and sated belches. He allowed the bear in
because he loved her. Because he no longer loved her.
Because he did not expect the bear to take to water,
paddling after his boat in a slough fog,
hungry for the back of his head.

Divinations

A Polaroid portrait, Janie's buoyant smile,
eyes closed, head tilt dramatic into empty sky,
a fading creased survivor from 1974—
I place this on a table beside the handful of

multicolor river stones pocketed on an Arizona
reservation in 2004. I pick up a pen, pause,
listening, *allegro moderato*, Sibelius, Violin
Concerto in D minor. A Sunday morning rises

inside me, days and years and rainstorms, a
slender white vase holding a single sunflower.
Back in my apartment, 1979, I am furiously
painting in dreamy afternoon sunshine, and Janie

does not suspect, for neither do I, that I am
painting the rugged road through treacherous
mountain terrain that leads me first to madness,
then to divorce, now to this window overlooking

an amiable grass, a venerable mulberry tree,
these six chattering ravens on a lax fence.

The Counterweight

He doesn't know.
His friend writes a book to him,
names it *Wounded Bear*,
       each poem a soft bullet through the paunch.
The Bear asleep beneath his assumptions.
The Bear dreaming of an escape, in the name of Love.
But, he doesn't know.
This is a friend with a secret he can never believe,
       in the endogenous winter
       behind the heart's lodge,
       snow-glowered,
birds of the wood warbling the cantata of dark animals.
Who is it keening over a Wounded Bear.
A friend.
She writes in a letter:
counterweight to a vast, sad, damned world.

Wrecked Sonnet

I wrecked my car in Moreno Valley watching
wild donkeys amble the streets beneath
jalapeño Christmas lights. I told the cop, No harm
no foul. How many dog barks will you hear in a lifetime.
That's how much truth you'll never catch. Do we
blame society for our faults, or is it the other way round.
I dig listening to ambient music—it's like calm dead people
in my brain. Shall we pour another scotch. Shall we
wipe the tears of grace from each other's faces.
Money is the antenna everywhere I go. Leaves
on the windshield, dirty pennies in the cupholder,
ladders falling off the back of trucks on the freeway.
As if having a thought is not a wrecked vehicle in itself.

This Sunday Feeling

this feeling is a little bear
sunday morning alone at a café table reading frank o'hara
i am going to touch in difficult ways
i am already exhausted with cruel pages of thought
i am skinny with self esteem
it is work to avoid acting like a horrible asshole
it is harder work because people i adore adore horrible assholes
it is prison labor to write a poem that's not a famished mammal
i am faking hibernation in an anxious cave
i am truly fucked if i can't even believe in my own afternoons
i am obese with self hatred
sunday evening alone at the kitchen table reading larry levis
this feeling is a lot of death

*The construction of this piece was born by playing with poem
titles from Tao Lin's *this emotion was a little e-book*.

No Elegance

I'd noticed the flimsy clutch
of carnations at the diner. Now
it's two-thirty in the morning,
on a fatigued motel bed: we're

trapped in Tehachapi. Yellow
carnations. Because you looked
collapsed. The whole diner
collected in one rose-colored

glass vase, drooping a little
under the hot silence. Three
in the morning, a train rumbles
along outside, a dog barks

down the street, you and me,
and from the window a blue
throw of neon that warms your
naked breath. Darkness hidden.

We've got honest, common
tragedies in bed with us, but
velveteen, their cumbersome
freight lifted for now—we

embraced when we got up
to leave the diner, large, tight,
unexpected, and here a window
pane collects us for the moon

to view with lazy grey eyes.
We are not mortals in these
pacified hours. Maybe naïve,
or ethereal, or fully bloomed,

I can't say, but I know there's
no elegance that compares to
this awkward grace, delicate
as it rests in our coarse hands.

IV. A distant wind-chime jitters

A Kind of Hum

That time when I took a train south through a western night sky,
all night it seemed, crossing coastal bridges, gliding gulls
in the window, stars phosphorescent, dropped like rhinestones
in the backlit surf, tracks clacking beneath cloud-lets
of cigarette smoke trapped in my dim compartment, with
strangers disinterested & silent, except a woman, humming,
& it was familiar, salient, the tune of her voice, but still today
I can't place it, though I can hear her as clear as my mother saying
Honey, everyone wants to be something to write home about, though
I never did & then Mom was gone, just like the lovely girl I was
riding that train to get to, longing to be even a sub-plot in her story,
but youth is a pair of scissors thinking it can rearrange anything
in any way, snip out obstacle or inconvenience, the holes
letting your shadows in, & what if I said you are made of
all the things you don't understand, clever caged bird, what if all
the duct tape, cracked windows, bitten lips, abandoned
puppies, boarded shops, dirty snow, dying trees, spent winds
& uneaten midnight-diner cherry pies on the long road back to
the home you can't ever get to, what if these wet red brake lights
in the dark are a kind of hum you're supposed to know, yet
here you are fluttering in the rattling train car of a memory
destined to extinction, no history or high mass: dulcet loneliness.

Poem Ending with a Barry Humphries Quote

You think you're the Ang Lee character who hears
a melody from a barking dog. A dog is still a dog.

A dial tone presages the movie full of dread and
technology. You think you'd like to watch your ex-

therapist-girlfriend crush karaoke with some crows
and a beat box, but The Answer is only an answer

if the right question has been posed, and a toy ship
can hold just as many ghosts as The Titanic.

If you see children through the window, if you
smell freshly-cut pears, if you hear plaintive violin

strings in the wind-blown curtain, and still your
point is illegibility, then your days are paragraphs

of dust. Do you laugh at yourself? Because if not,
my friend, you're missing the joke of the century.

Muse

My boyfriend strums darker than a Blue Period guitar
abandoned in a Bohemian café. In the rain.

Tonight, my sister and I will let down the dark curtain of our hair.
My husband will watch me with wet Labrador eyes,

then when she and I step out, the city night will brush our faces
like hummingbird wings, and before long my boyfriend's darkness

will fly through my body. I'll pet his cats as I leave.
My sister will nest until daylight with her coffeehouse waitress.

When she and I return, my husband will jump in my lap again
and re-marry me, again, in an even darker dream.

Poem with Little Riffs on Oscar Wilde, Ann Leshy Wood, Lisa Marr, and Some Memes

Poetry is not tribalism. Communist jokes
are not funny unless everyone tells them.

Poetry is too important to be taken seriously.
Take a moment for joy— poems are

blunder blessing and found fortune. Mine
also "strange little music boxes."

Their imperfections are my greatest asset
in a digital world where calculated

indignation is the new sincerity.
The online self is a curated self.

The poem, also, is a curated self.
I don't know why I'm here. You can't

explain a poem— you have to witness it.
Social media exists and time is not

going to kill itself: Pat Robertson flails
and rails about Obama lesbian witches.

Liberty versus Industry: you know who wins.
Maybe this poem is a monkey from the future.

Maybe the future is pretty pissed off.
Meanwhile, a pasture dreams of horses.

Meanwhile, the negative effect of using
marijuana... is having less marijuana.

But we will not take stones for eyes!
Weighing over four hundred pounds,

this is the heart of a blue whale. Or a gravy
hot tub at the White-is-Right

Motor Inn. Now you see: I've always
been my own worst enemy. I cruise

down to Rancho Cucamonga
to photograph suburban ghosts

and homeless street preachers.
My safety word is "harder." Nobody came

here tonight to watch me write poems
that don't matter for people who shatter

endlessly. Poetry is not tribalism.
And I am the Velvet Elvis in this poem.

Healing

Outside,
September Mojave wind
moans for Miles,
but it only wants the air
in my house
to blow through my skull
like that genius of indifference
through his horn.
Wind only understands wind.

Instead,
I need to play Etta James.
I'd clasp a diamond necklace
around her neck, take her
out to a little Creole joint I know
in Palmdale.

She'd wink across the table,
wipe etouffee
with a paper napkin, say
All you ever got to do to find soul food
is keep the rhythm of things
with your body.

She'd be radiant,
but I wouldn't make a pass.
You see,
I'm the sugar-powder buddha
in her warm beignet
just waiting to be eaten.

I can't invent my music
by brute force, or live the
field hand gospel
of womanhood, but I know enough—

the wind's bitter conceit,
the kitchen's savory fire.
We have only a brief time to feel
what notes we can play
in this world.

Every Damn Thing

Was it angels or devils that tortured Frida, is what I've
wondered, or sometimes whether stars are too far away

to be looking at. You were always either micropolitically
upholstered like some Bernadette Mayer sonnet or slipping

in 'n out like blue smoke from Miles' trumpet, but I digress.
Once Frida had a stake driven through her she never had to

pretend again (poor Diego always envious of this). I've
pulled peregrine, sliver, brushfire, shrine, numinous jazzy

scats from down inside, even what felt like fish-hook, but
let's come back to what I'll never know: which is what

parts of me are pretending, what parts are disappearing,
what parts know my self better than you knew me. I hate

that I had a nice day today because when your mother died
I became a pornographic magazine of actors' empathy. I felt

tremorous hurt hurtling down, rocks on your mountain road,
but all that could be done was catch them, show them to you,

convince you to call them by different names: igneous
for anger, sediment for sadness, metamorphous for self-

loathing. Did what men do: feverishly fuck and explain for
as long as he hasn't a clue. Every mask I could make im-

paled on highest stakes: what I got for trying to be right
about every damn thing, instead of being a self in love.

An Inventory of Hunger

A Girl in Seashell Teeth Stopped Him Thinking

With her, he just knew. Could see dry land through sea-green eyes. Kisses like tides, rolling him into her secret cove. He opened lips like sails on smiles, and when she ebbed, he fell, then flowed.

She Tries to Live in a Cave

I'm in, for whole life. Even want to thank you, mizzly night, as I prepare his favorite meal: soft-boiled, long-tail regret. At home, in the waterfall. Startled between sweet and funny, blame topples from him, rock slides, everything bad that's ever happened since Adam&Eve screwed, and now, steaming in mango morning light, we're carrying all the rain that falls out of all the trees.

He Figures a Way Out

I've been relative (r) between California and Indiana (c/i), plus theoretically wherever she's tried to be (t*x). By my calculations, distance went exponential (wtf) and speed desynchronized to sleep (zzz) ;;; her curving wide right or pulling hairpin left nothing but a circle closing. Turns out my math was off. We've never been near a solution.

Self-Portrait with a Woman

Madison explains a dare over shots in a San Diego bar. Before even that, I want inside her, and it's like my nude photographic idea of Frida talking back to me, reading me a hand-painted note. Unfolded napkin of green fronds, open breasts, black monkeys and hearts, stained by failed bodies and cigarettes—the how and where of sex in this shattered skin.

Never at Peace

It's not half that easy to be uneasy. No to yoga and long lazy hikes. No pan flute downloads to her iPhone, no sandals on her feet. Refuses to cuddle her sister's puppies, or vegans or chocolate or even green tea. Self-help? Mockery. So's total calm. Naps are permitted, but only in the realm of extramarital lovers, men she saves like coupons. She redeems them with her troubles, has never slept so lonely.

Camera Lux

The photograph is scuffed. She is perfect and visible. There is a horse tangled in her hair. It will be two years yet before it escapes. She doesn't know, though she is smiling out to you from within the picture's pool, she doesn't know yet whether next week she'll have grown or shrunk by twenty feet, but she knows size is always shifting, and she knows light makes image possible. If the mind is a moonlit room. A wall, a door, a dresser. Your favorite shirt draped over her chair. One half of the room, cut away diagonally. The room's other half weighed down by black corners, floor nearly tilting.

Love Poems, Grace

I:

Desert wind at sunset, broken town where flags pull apart,
reaching out for water. Buoy clang of flagpole from the old stables.
Skyline steeped orange on platinum,
the few trees holding their leaves, open sails
against a Mojave autumn. Roots pull up for sunlight.
My phone keeps ringing, as if it has something to say.
Two women, on a palomino and a paint, amble past blistered fence rails.
Their horses smell the cold sea rising, air tense with it,
wind swinging wide open a pearled flood of night.

II:

Her sentences a perfume,
gardenias, strong and sweet and almost overpowering.
All I can do not to stare at the music flickering in her eyes.
I want to lie in a green field after light rain,

feel her lips making animal shapes from bright clouds.
I want to hold my palm against her cheek, caress her humming.
I want to taste her singing into deaf night.
I want to lean into her neck, the flower of her breath.

Dreams are for later, when the lights are out,
everyone else asleep.

III:

San Francisco coffee house, September rain.
Krishnamurti's on the radio, his voice weaving
between intermittent bursts of Coltrane, espresso screams,
and Bonnie, who whispers to me from across the table. I listen
as if within the walls of a Vienna opera house, listening
as Mozart must have. Bonnie wears perfect

gold shoes. Her syllables drape the caffeine steam.
"Our thinking cannot solve our problems," Krishnamurti says,
and the warm needle of those words threads
into my bones. Somewhere someone is dying, someone else
falling in love again. Here it is San Francisco, the sea leaning,
without intent, and it is raining, cool. Bonnie sips cappuccino
in a late afternoon lull, the full lotus bloom of desire.

Maybe, Maybe

I might find another dog. Maybe next year, after I've finished
with this year's therapist, done with all that talking about the
unsuccessful talking I've done with other people, maybe I'll be
stripped down to just walking or sitting and saying *Good dog!*

There's a kind of immortality to my dreams and it feels like
those so-called eternal moments when dreaming I am running
and laughing with Rusty or Fiona, good dogs, good dogs, loyal
and loving, or at least I believe in it being real, tangible, reliable,

and it occurs to me maybe I've failed in that kind of willingness
to believe when it comes to humans. When the heart dies it's a
foreboding riddle, when the brain dies it's Merry Christmas,
everything distilled down to your childhood, be it happy or sad,

peppermint or coal, and in yesterday's session I remembered
taking Rusty to the "home" my great grandmother had been
remanded to when in 1972 she woke up in 1944 and liked it so
much she stayed. Rusty understood boyhood, disliked my father,

and instantly befriended Nano that afternoon. We sat with her
for hours saying next to nothing, just handholding and smiling.
Later in the 70s I'd be wrecked by booze, acid, coke, merciless
friends and lovers, and so-so-so many lies, so much smack talk,

back talk, back stabs and cash grabs, and I paid less attention
to Rusty, then he died and I got confused, climbed a mountain,
laid in the cold wet grass alone to sleep for years and years—
at last got up, descended, looked for some river to float down.

I found a stray, called her Fiona! She adopted me and next
thing you know I stopped talking and found a human who said
I love you. I was with Fiona while she died and told her *I've
told you everything I could never tell anyone,* and she knew,

she knew. Said none of this to my therapist. Maybe next year
will be the year, another year of silence with a one-man dog.

Inevitable

Horses take anything goes: sweet carrot, earthy alfalfa,
damn fool with a hat & saddle.

It's not like fearless,
        more like dance— moving to feel life rush in
without being an obvious target.

        At middle school hops, I stood against the dark
gym wall to gawk at Julie's

baby face while she shimmied across a lit floor.
        I wasn't scared, just struck by lightning, frozen

        by the heat of her hips.

I could have run to the pasture of the parking lot when
        she turned a smile directly through me,
but I had a head full of hope,

lunged by a boy's dream & awkward Hully Gully moves.

So that's the dance—
look at me, you can't have me, well okay maybe. I like
turning my horses out in early morning,

how they run right at the widening mouth of horizon.
        I like my clumsy dance, my
rough ride, the inevitable kicks & falls & forgiveness.

Covid Spring

She hated spring coming—
So full of death, she said.

Martyred by the explosion of life, I replied.

It was a time of novel coronavirus,
our sickly cats,
and baby bunnies orphaned in hay bales,
their mothers flattened on the road around the barn.

It was a time of elegy,
America dying right before our eyes
like a young, gargantuan, colicky stallion.

There was a magical desperate quality to everything.

Some morning would come, surely,
to prove it all a dream,
but we hardly slept, and never past four-thirty a.m.

I'm thinking of that high school summer now,
climbing down a jagged
Baja California cliff to the shore at midnight,
seeing sand sharks in the water,

smoking some weed,
sleeping beneath a lunar eclipse.

I'm thinking about the soul of a horse
and the hole it leaves
when his body abandons him.

When she comes to me, in grief or in joy, it is this
coming of spring—I take
the fullness of life and death equal, magical
and desperate,

we together alone, where we ache with the same
animal soul, wash in the same ocean of night,

moon-bathed, broken and healed,
a little afraid, but always ready.

Intervals and Rhythms

How does it feel? Comfortable
       but edgy.
Political and artistic. Fall and spring.
Nobody can make rent,
even in this rusty little desert town, and nobody has spaces,
so we cobble together outdoors, with or without mics,
behind coffee shops and used book stores, passing around flasks
of old bourbon, to project our poems—
       cultures and saints, universities
       and friends. My awful writing is solid, my detachment
a smolder of wisen'd ash,
sooty, with this long, low breath of cello steadily rising
to sound this homeless shelter or that prison
or maybe my uninhabited childhood.
There are a lot of writers,
and *There's no such thing as bad writing!* says Dorothea Lasky.
There *is* a shortage of people worth listening to, say I—
musicians and yogi, also, of this same cloth. I am not here to
liberate or be liberated. Collaborate, yes,
       on a raga of poetry, infinity, exigency.
       See, I've lived through
blackouts and plagues, witnessed death—
       I want,
I want a touch so bewitching that it haunts me forever.

Forgive Us All

Split lip from falling over a footstool
 with three fingers of Johnnie Walker in a crystal rocks glass
  I bought on Amazon, blue Christmas Eve.
Got cleaned up by lunch.
 Had those vagrant-red, goose-lid eyes you see on TV
in beaten downtown bars where everyone drinks
  Kessler or Ten High.

My boss's son was murdered by white supremacists at Cal State.

Everything frosted over in the morning.
I slowed down, ate too much rich food, stopped trying.
 My wife was happy to have her sickly mother to worry about
  instead of me.
Time is a trick.

This toothsome, sixty-something black guy
 with a bushy moustache,
  wearing a seven-spiked crown and a pink prom dress,
leaned out a passing car window to shout
   I say yes! I forgive you all!, then blew me a kiss.

Remember Miss Liberty, she said, riding into sunrise.

When the moon was fat that bright white morning
  I walked right through the muscle of her pink breath.
She's on the river's other side,
  where I can see horses and passerines,
 wild blue sweetclover.
  I keep calling up strength to make the swim over.
Same moon at night.
    There is no sleep outside her,
her a cracked bell, with the drag queen clapper.

Messenger Without Umbrella

The generous puddle that grows in our driveway
from leaky sprinklers
looks like a hole full of stars tonight—

magnetic splurge, burning ark, I feel hope.

Not the greeting card variety, more a murmur,
a nanosecond of gentle, elemental fire.

Ashes to ashes, dust to dust, that's the stuff
of eternity, & so I am. Eternal.

Don't bother to try & get at the "I."
Alan Watts said "Trying to define yourself

is like trying to bite your own teeth."

That's a crater full of stars, too, a jaw gnawing at
supernovas & black holes. That's

chasing the idea of self. I don't believe in whispers
or wet umbrellas, don't believe in belief.

The little blue-white lights in this accidental
pool seem a piece of
chance advice, by way of Duchamp, perhaps.

Marcel would ask, "Did you know God's mother
was a hairdresser?" & I'd say

No, but it figures. My
grandmother was a red-haired universe &
she managed her own salon for nearly fifty years.

Weathered

& we remained
                    it wasn't too late
                              spilling air
We talked about   what Buddha meant
                    in the stagnant night
Going back to our women   he said
                              In our underwear
The watermelon eating fizzing stars &
                    global warming before us
                    we were sixty-three
on the wooden chairs   silent &
                    California was
                    drying up
On an Echo Park stoop he & I sat
                              It was the summer
he had the chemo   hoping for a breeze
                    It was the summer lawn
                    turned to straw & we were
burning down   side by side
                              He told me
O the watermelon   how sweet & icy it was

Horse Sense

You can tell a horse anything.
Barn swallows scatter from rafters
in high-throated song when you open your mouth,
but a horse listens just right.
      Such is the nonchalance of the stall. Outside,
the riverbed fills with blue fog this morning, and I run a brush
through the white mare's winter coat,
my stories streaming through her ear, and what a luxury for us both:
      to not have a common language,
to not let subtleties dam the way of understanding. I can't see the
scrub along the riverbank, only the shape waters have worn
into the earth, and glassy eyes of houses from the other side
glaring down at everything untamed.
      Some things hidden are best not discovered.
Some days best begin just brushing your horse in a fog.

Poem in which I Survive

I wake wondering why I am horizontal on my birthday,
sixty-seventh, more shortcomings than there are grasshoppers
in summer, more ambitions squandered than Bukowski.
My bed may as well be a coffin. Even moonlight avoids it.
At the Dollar General, I buy two six-packs of Korean beer
to celebrate my doctor's misdiagnosis, and I notice
hummingbirds, of all things, wavering near a feeder wired
inexplicably onto the side of an awning, wings braiding
the parking lot air, where a little sunlight has just begun
to leak from the sky. Somewhere right now masses, devoid
of contrition, are praying for the strength to destroy those
who thirst, those who survive by eating fourteen crisp, green
grasshoppers a day— I will not surrender. Will not give up
the Chalice of Hope. I can be two parts sugar, one part water.

Night Whispers

I've been hidden way the hell out here,
a hundred-plus miles northeast of Los Angeles,
in a breathtaking stupor among the locals,
everyone with sand in their hair
and in their scuffed leather boots.
It's a beautiful summer night in the Mojave,

though no one is listening to the low lecture
of the hills and the river—humming
a warm breeze, interspersed with
the burble of nighthawks. What does it matter?
Circa 1875, everyone in the City of Angels
knew one another, or at least their families.

There were no such class distinctions
as we have today. Now it's midnight
in early August and everybody in that flat
city is alone. Out here, the stars
flirt with me, and I'll pour an iced tea, slide
the flesh of a fresh lemon wedge onto the lip

of my glass, make a call to a friend
and talk about my tumor, as the old
adobe cools among moonlit Joshua Trees.
This desert by day tells so many lies you
have to write them down to keep them straight.
Night whispers terrible truths about spring.

I have no faith without you, your ten-gallon

appetite, your drunken slide into convolution,
my nervous system as your tongue and fingers
glow my body like a Santa Barbara palm in a
money-to-burn conflagration. I'm always in a
black market for love with you. Always an itch.
We got hitched and called ourselves senseless.
Joke's on us: we're trapped in this silken pond,
floating with citrus rinds, under a circus tent
that rhymes with resilient. Beseeming—Satis.

Whichever god tried to curse us is bewildered.

Post-Pandemic Spring

It is spring again, Love,
      and the earth has gone insane
      with color and scent.
We will be lulled,
      forgetting death,
and a forgetting of branches quivering in a wind,
      or land under fall of snow,
or bleak sky
against which we knew the small deaths
      that told of all the separate deaths
we must dream alone.

Look, Love, at the lilac
and the dog rose, look at the fledgling waking up
to the world,
      a cluster of May blossoms,
look at each tree create its own peculiar shape
      of leaf,
      each knowing which form to take,
its part in a twelve-act tragedy
      scripted in seed.

Look, Love, this rising of sap
      is not new.
We have known it before, a prelude
      to all our summers.
This is the growth of light
      and the diminishment of fear.
Through silver pools and under birch we walk,
      as the sun drops
warm kisses in our hands—

and at night among the lush sheets we spend
      our hoarded selves
and lose in the forgetting

and lose in the rising
this knowledge
that the path grows shorter in the greening year.

Come from the Blinding Light and Hear

Let me tell you about the riotous golden rock-daisy
bloom along the riverbank and how no one can
get enough of the new mare. You'd go gaga over her.

Blue, gray, and white scrub-jays have nested in
the sugar bush. This morning I watched them collect
shiny objects to stash in their twigs. As of today,

our chitchat has been a clandestine language for
twenty-two years. Out loud or by way of pen, words
snagged in my throat, flesh on barbed wire. Until now.

I still feel your palm in mine when you slipped away,
see the fear in your morphine-doused eyes when
the moment came. Your voice is clear, though you've

revealed zero about kingdom come. That's okay.
I garden, even tend the roses for you, have no fear of
horses and listen to every sort of bird for news of

spring. Let me tell you about your great grandson's
smile, his eyes, how he dozes swathed in my arms.
I whisper your name, secretly, in his immaculate ear.

Screwy Rabbits

My White Rabbit was a hundred rabbits, a hundred habits
still, a thousand more in waiting. Who was it that said,

If you want everything you get nothing? No one I know,
maybe should have been me. When I was 12 it was boobs,

stolen beers from the fridge. At 17, it was Lu Ann, life
as an L.A. muralist, half a kilo in the freezer. 23 brought

thoughts of escape, divorce by fake suicide underneath
the bridge. 32, renewed, a Buddhist with six girlfriends,

no money, writing all day and night on coffee and whiskey,
wrote my way into professorship, tenure, raising a great

kid with a great lady, me now the hippy-dippy grandpa.
But there's been a million stops or detours along this

path, held together by tragedy and joy, shrooms and toys,
a lot of a lot of falling in love with a lot of, well,

visons and girls and music and poems and this sweeping
delusion of peace, art, sex, sleep, falling light as an

autumn leaf to decompose—pure beauty in the breakdown.

Grief is a Coat

I made myself a promise: No to death in Alabama,
no Mexican divorce. No Trotsky face, despite my Frida-esque
tendencies. No more ordinary. Only strange!
Maybe I'm a missing link, maybe a commie,
but surely a noble scene sans Spandex, sans violence,
suffering from too many red tulips, not enough bites at a fresh
green apple. Alack and alas, I feel a sleep-walking mermaid
in my future. I feel my mother's kiss and a dream shaped like
Buddhism. The question is: How do you feel?
How's it going and do you want to talk about it?
I've had enough of absence. Let's get vivid, full of oxygen—
let's say all of us for all of us, because that bears a striking
resemblance to the life we thought we wanted.
My mother's wild brilliant ghost keeps saying
Grief is a coat you only give away to the best of best friends.

Let's Crash

It's Lou Reed's birthday, so I put on Laurie Anderson's
Heart of a Dog, have a good cry for all my animals in their

selfless deaths, echoes of my helplessness in both ears—
how I searched their faces while little black clouds

settled in their eyes. I'm sticking my tongue down the
throat of the Bardo. Sometimes I think like Los Angeles,

though more Echo Park than Santa Monica. Actually, a
hot afternoon solo on Pico at *Tacos El Tamix*, gorging in

silence on their alambre (a hash of sautéed al pastor, chili
peppers, onions, bacon, and Oaxacan cheese), tastes pretty

lonesome, too, like how Roy Orbison always looked secretly
sad even when singing about beautiful women. I know these

liquor stores, graffitied churches, and smog-choked palms,
Porsches, porches, Adderall, flea markets, knives, guns,

rape spray, straight or gay, Chinese New Years taking
both wallet and breath away, movie stars you think you'd

like to meet, Venus as a boy down an unlit street, from
the valley to the hood, city misunderstood, city disguised

as a body made from Mexican Korea Town and Rich
White Ghettos, its histories knotted like the veins of a

Tarantino speedball mock-umentary, with us the blood to
both brain and asshole, doped expansive on rock 'n roll

'n race, nourishing this body without a face. On second
thought, let's do Santa Monica, let's crash *Chez Jay*, do an

Angus steak, and after all the martinis and hot bourbon
shots it will be, of a sudden, last call—we'll amble into a

two-a.m. fog that skims the arc-light street as we circle
block after block, forgetting where we parked our lives.

California Love Song

Yes, I'll say yes to another new bloom,
another coastal-mountainous-desert bouquet

of blissful sun flowering, even though
so many of my best friends are done with it,

choosing to live outside the discomfort of
change, and steep tax on sedentary thinking.

My own Restlessness, faithful companion,
pleads to move someplace, too, but I say

this is my native soil! Maybe I'd be doing
great in a different city. Maybe the blossoms

of some faraway field would be ambrosial,
but that's saccharine dreaminess—what I

need is ample space for greatness, no matter
the weakness of my gardening, so I keep

making pots and plots, and I'll keep planting.
Roots take hold, sprouts, then stems, so yes,

I'm happy to settle for one new leaf. Water
and prune, mulch and compost, plus plenty of

honest shit, and so it grows: a usable version
of truth, in one of beauty's fetid guises. I'm

never giving up on my chances to come home
right here, in poppies and disappointment.

Family

It's Friday night at the Headless Horseman.
Gypsies and Indians career to the floor,

bone-yard pairs in marigold, dancing and
drunk, beat and hooting, their hard faces lifting

in the yellow light that bathes the warp-wood
platform, as next door novena's million candles

flicker in the weary apse of Our Lady of Infinite
Sadness. Soon, the haggard band will disappear,

packing their hoarse notes and dead-lover lyrics
into a creased pickup truck, speeding and jostling

across the pitch-bleak desert bed, tossing
bottles of beer at hopes that flit like rabbits

in the road. But for now, the room is jump and
smoke and smile. Julio and Nadine are back

together, Sal buys Jack a whiskey, making up for
last Thursday's busted nose. Henry sputters near

the juke, hands clammy, the flick of his tongue
feeling like wet carpet in his mouth, while

Jo Maria, dark and frowning as always, pays him
all the attention in the world by paying almost

no attention to him at all. How everyone needs
one another. How everyone wants not to. How

beautiful strange when all our skeletons gather,
like family, out here where coyote winds dog

the mid-June night, while a distant wind-chime jitters, shaking music from the angry air.

About the Author

Michael Dwayne Smith lives near a ghost town in the Mojave Desert with his wife, rescued horses, and Calamity the California calico cat. He is the author of five books, *Shaking Music from the Angry Air* being his fourth. He's a recipient of both the Hinderaker Poetry Prize and the Polonsky Prize for fiction; recent award nominations include three for the Pushcart Prize, three for Best of the Net, and one for the StorySouth Million Writers Award. His work appears in more than three hundred journals, magazines, anthologies, textbooks, and newspapers around the world, including *The Cortland Review, Gargoyle, Third Wednesday, Heron Tree, Star 82 Review, New World Writing Quarterly, Superstition Review, Monkeybicycle, Chiron Review, San Pedro River Review,* and *Heavy Feather Review*. He is Professor Emeritus of Education and Educational Technology at Victor Valley College, and, when not writing or teaching, he serves as publisher/editor-in-chief of *Mojave River Press & Review*; he's also served as editor-in-chief of the literary journals *Cease, Cows* and *Mosaic*, as guest editor of *Cholla Needles Literary Journal*, and as a judge for the Dogfish Head Poetry Prize in book-length collections.

Sheila-Na-Gig Editions

www.ingramcontent.com/pod-product-compliance
Lightning Source LLC
Chambersburg PA
CBHW031421120626
46545CB00006B/2212